It All
Changed
in an
Instant

Not Quite What I Was Planning: Six-Word

   Memoirs by Writers Famous & Obscure

Six-Word Memoirs on Love & Heartbreak

I Can't Keep My Own Secrets: Six-Word

   Memoirs by Teens Famous & Obscure

It All Changed in an Instant

More Six-Word Memoirs by
Writers Famous & Obscure
From SMITH Magazine
Edited by Rachel Fershleiser
and Larry Smith

HARPER  PERENNIAL

NEW YORK • LONDON • TORONTO • SYDNEY • NEW DELHI • AUCKLAND

HARPER ● PERENNIAL

HarperCollins books may be purchased for educational, business, or sales promotional use. For information please write: Special Markets Department, HarperCollins Publishers, 10 East 53rd Street, New York, NY 10022.

FIRST HARPER PERENNIAL EDITION PUBLISHED 2010.

Designed by Justin Dodd

Library of Congress Cataloging-in-Publication Data is available upon request.

ISBN 978-0-06-171943-1

10 11 12 13 14 OV/RRD 10 9 8 7 6 5 4 3 2 1

Introduction

"For sale: baby shoes, never worn."
> —Ernest Hemingway, American writer

"It all changed in an instant."
> —Candis Sykes, accounting-group leader
> and American writer

Legend has it that the short-short story came about in a bar bet when Ernest Hemingway was challenged to write a novel in only six words. We'll probably never know whether the anecdote is factual or apocryphal, but we do know this: the challenge works. Three years ago, on the storytelling Web site SMITH Magazine, we gave the classic form a contemporary twist. In these confessional times, we wondered if people could use six words to tell the true story of their own lives. Since then, more than 250,000 six-word memoirs have been submitted to

SMITH Magazine (SMITHMag.net) and its younger cousin, SMITH Teens (SMITHteens.com).

We've published three books of these life stories so far, *Not Quite What I Was Planning*, *Six-Word Memoirs on Love & Heartbreak*, and *I Can't Keep My Own Secrets*. The response from readers, writers, librarians, teachers, artists, parents, and children has blown us away. Preachers and rabbis alike have embraced six-word prayers. In hospitals and shelters, from after-school programs to speed dating, six-word memoirs have been used to ease communication, foster understanding, and break the ice. A SMITH contributor who goes by the screen name "Miandering" documented her year of traveling the globe in a series of more than 100 six-word memoirs submitted one by one—*"Sticky rice at every meal. Yum"* (a great start in Thailand) to *"Wet flip-flops. Shiny linoleum. Bad combination"* (a tough break in Malaysia). Teachers from kindergarten to graduate school have found the six-word memoir an inspiring writing lesson. In a third-grade classroom in New Jersey, we heard *"Life is better in soft pajamas"* and one student's precocious Zen observation: *"Tried surfing on a calm day."*

Like our first book, *Not Quite What I Was Planning: Six-Word Memoirs by Writers Famous & Obscure,* the one you're holding offers a mix of bestselling memoirists like the late Frank McCourt (*"The miserable childhood leads to royalties"*) and debut writers like Jennifer Labbienti (*"I still practice my Oscar speech"*). There are stories from the iconic and visionary Gloria Steinem (*"Life is one big editorial meeting"*) and the unfamous and practical Joy Zuercher (*"Can't reach top shelves, married tall"*). We're confident you'll find all our storytellers equally worthwhile, but if being published alongside Pulitzer Prize winners like Junot Díaz and Tony Kushner validates any aspiring authors, all the better.

And just as we like to balance populist and aspirational, we see six words as both complete and open-ended. It's plenty to tell an entire story, but it's often just the start. We've heard from many people whose six-word creations spurred them to shoot for six hundred, six thousand, or more. Robin Templeton, author of *"After Harvard, had baby with crackhead,"* the first story in our first book, is now working on a full-length memoir. In that spirit, we've added a feature called "backstory" on SMITHmag.net, where you can tell the longer tale behind your mini-memoir. And this book features an appendix, where, for the first time, we've included a selection of stories behind the six. (Six-word purists should feel free to skip that part.) Online there are many more backstories, as well as art and videos from contributors all over the world.

We launched SMITH Magazine to provide a new kind of reading experience, a place where users create the content and editors curate it. The success of the Six-Word Memoir project proved that people are hungry for passionate personal stories, told in a forum where everyone is welcome and the literary playing field is level. This book contains less than 1 percent of the torrent of self-expression that arrives at our virtual doorstep each day. If you're new here, we welcome you to our world of six, and hope you'll head over to sixwordmemoirs.com to claim your place in it. We can even send you our pick for the Six-Word Memoir of the Day via Twitter, the microblogging platform that has exploded since the tech wizards there helped launch the first six-word memoir contest back in 2006.

With each submission, our library of shared stories becomes wider, deeper, and richer. The growth of a small writing game into an international phenomenon is definitely not quite what we were planning, but it's incredibly gratifying. And if there's one thing we've learned never to doubt, it's this: It really can all change in an instant.

> **Larry Smith** ("Now I obsessively count the words.")
> and
> **Rachel Fershleiser** ("Morning: national television. Afternoon: bookstore bathrooms.")
> September 2009, New York City

It All
Changed
in an
Instant

I just hope there's a sequel.

—Lila Louise Nawrocki

**Writing is easy.
Life is hard.**

—Neil LaBute

NEARING 60,
STILL ON ROUGH DRAFT.

—Sydney Smith Zvara

My life made
my therapist laugh.

—Isabel Lara

Zip. Zero. Zilch.
Nothing published. Yet.

—Beth Carter

Lost virginity in white van.
Irony?

—Tricia Van der Grient

Programmer,
impresario,
lawyer;
name still girly.

—Lindsay Bowen, Jr.

My self image is Indiana Jones.

—Christopher Day

No siblings means complicated
adult relationships.

—Jamie Denbo

Peed on White House
floor. Really.

—Phil Jacobsen

Friendship test:
willingness
to be inconvenienced.

—Gay Talese

We honeymooned in
    California divorce court.

—Atalie Kessler

Antidepressants ruined
emo music for me.

—Lucy Waters

The slot machine, my reverse ATM.

—Henry Penland

*Dancing through life
in sensible shoes.*

—Gaylene Meyer

That homeless man
is my stepfather.

—Oubria Tronshaw

Stripper then,
sexual abuse therapist now.

—Megan Blair

Wake. Bathe. Work. Eat. Sleep.
Repeat.

—Shane Kittelson

Cramps have ruined my whole life.

—Aime Marie Easton

Stole my stuff,
not my memories.

—Paula R. Parker

You don't age while
viewing beauty.

—Sammy Hagar

Learned to draw with my foot.

—Chelsea Hadley

JOURNALISM MAJOR:
NOT AFRAID OF DEATH.

—Lisa Qiu

High school art teacher. MFA wasted.

—Brian Harmon

My soulmates are all gay men.

—Denise Brennan

**Big boobs, short waist,
great gams.**

—Allison Hemming

The upside of Alzheimer's: "new" mother.

—Susan Cushman

First love lost, 14; married, 50.

—Joyce Mason

I spell God
with two o's.

—Jon Schulberg

Writing's my escape. Pills were hers.

—Catherine Maynard

Sent home.
Baby born in bathtub.

—Anita Hahn

World of Warcraft stole my life.

—Brooks Glass

Still trying to outrun the Baptists.

—Leslie Hill

Got degree, lost job, happy homemaking.

—Kimberly Weisberg

Foster parent.
I now know heartbreak.

—Colleen Sprague

Succeeded in forgiving;
failed to forget.

—Denise Diaz

```
ARMY OR JAIL?
I CHOSE WRONG.
```

—Peter Loux

Former boss: "Writing's

your worst skill!"

—Amy Tan

White girl, tragically hip,
misses mountains.

—Jennifer Ratola

From acting to being!
Evolution rocks!

—Linus Roache

Loudest fan at son's
lacrosse game.

—Amy Hartl Sherman

Raise your glass,
lower your standards!

—Thom Filicia

404: Life could not be found.

—Ryan Hartkopf

Straight white male struggling
with privilege.

—Paul Brown

**FINALLY REACHED
THE TOP.
GOING DOWN.**

—Amelia Craver

**Leather-loving Indian
vegetarian, speaks ahimsa!**

—Pavitra Maragani

*Dancing alone;
pleased while others grimace.*

—Natasha J. Reed

Bralessness made me a bad girl.

—Laura Chase

Wedding dress lasted longer than husband.

—Jeannette Oliver

Born in wrong comic book universe.

—Tami Marshall

Public health nerd: I love condoms.

—Beth Linas

Stuck in a job
I love.

—Lori Lipkind

I hate this
Groundhog Day feeling.

—Nicole Reyes

My motto: Draw comics every day.

—Alec Longstreth

Was Irish-Italian Catholic. Now Jewish.

—Yisrael Campbell

Expected forever.
Have restraining order instead.

—Abbe Shapiro

PHILADELPHIA STORY:
VOLUNTEER DRIVER
MEETS EDITOR.

—Judith G. Goldman

I'm more Clark Kent than
Superman.

—Roger Sperry

Will finish novel after grading
papers.

—Jill Steinmetz

There are consequences to my color.

—Afua Richardson

Cloudy with a chance
of sun.

—Julie Beman

I'm a sucker for
a goatee.

—Ann McGinley

My rise to fame went
unnoticed.

—Steven Newman

Downward mobility
took me by
surprise.

—Crysta Kessler

Nothing rhymed, so I wrote haiku.

—Tanja Cilia

**Haven't worn a dress
since prom.**

—Lacy Foland

*Ring on finger,
question in heart.*

—Jessica Douglas-Monks

Never thought
I'd be producing
porn!

—Randy Johnson

Bad knees:
need cane at 20.

—Carolyn Bailey

Bachelor Party.

YouTube video.

Wedding cancelled.

—Daniel Little

Stranger in Sudan
made everything possible.

—Anthony Capstick

The best antidote?
Spontaneous
international
adventures.

—Jessi Hamel

Tiny son dying in my arms.

—Noema Abbott

Love blew the classroom doors off.

—Chance Hunt

I'll always need crutches.
Stop asking!

—Joy Griffin

—David Heatley

Tattoos made my skin more "me."

—Melissa Maxwell

**Always wished I could sing.
Biochemist.**

—Jen DuBois

*Broke rules. Dated coworker.
Blissfully married.*

—Meagan Swenson

**FROM LOW
BUDGET TO HIGH
MAINTENANCE.**

—Lisa Ihnken

Only I define who I am.

—Montel Williams

Loves box wine in Solo Cups.

—Maggie McDonald

Not "small town," yet from one.

—Amiee Blaisdell

I always really liked
leaving home.

—Isaac Fitzgerald

**Overworked artist
fantasizes about
DMV career.**

—Sara Boucher Rhodes

Six months, $20,000,
two miscarriages,
done.

—Kellie Wiegand

I was young . . .
    needed the money.

—Deb Nies

Belonging? Itineraries felt
safer than addresses.

—Tovli Simiryan

Ten years, 100,000 dollars:
indentured MD.

—Andrea Skaggs

*Wanted: stories heard on
mother's lap.*

—Tony Parsons

From pablum to prunes,
great trip.

—Rich Sanderson

Born
with
big
nose.
Pursued
comedy.

—Andy Borowitz

I Photoshopped out your worst features.

—Melissa Appleby

Same-sex marriage? Yup.
Lesbians divorced? Yup.

—H. M. Hegedus

Kitchen: public radio.
Bedroom: library books.

—Joy Franson

Caring for critters saved my sanity.

—Kelly Meister

Dad's funeral. Daughter's birth.
Flowers everywhere.

—Tiffany Shlain

From bar singer to Halloween costume.

—Taylor Hicks

Eat red meat, drink red wine.

—Marcy Gordon

I saw the Red Sox win.

—Tom Phillips

First comes love, then comes stalking.

—Jeff Metcho

Made weird children—will die proud.

—Rachel Pealer

Secretly happy I'm still a virgin.

—Randi Baron

Good friends. Bad diet. Ugly apartments.

—Joe Dungan

Straight-A student, now
flunking judgment.

—Miranda Kaplan

WHY WALK WHEN YOU CAN
FLY?

—Arturo Sandoval

Dragons slain, maidens
rescued, villains thwarted.

—Mike Burke

Married Russian. Brush teeth
with vodka.

—Curt Brandao

Unplanned but perfect:
Heather, Hannah, Haley.

—Lisa Kein

Found a boy 3,000 miles away.

—Stephanie Janusz

Born female, now male:
strange trip.

—Matt Kailey

Grandchildren's smiles—
no other mirrors needed.

—Aileen Brown

Pickles too sour,
life too sweet.

—Bryn Nolan

Used to live in a box.

—Ana Henry

Drank tequila. Barfed
asleep. Got divorced.

—Alan Hubbard

Raped, never forgave
myself, wasted life.

—Judith Currin

Drowning in diapers,
mac and cheese.

—Kay Cox

Obama: happiest
I've been in years.

—Deborah Schneider

Charlie and I are always posing.

–Kari Harendorf

Adopted from Peru, can't find parents.

—Nora Andors

I'm living better than billions, sadly.

—John Sheffield

Wanted independence
but had two dependents.

—Tara Lazar

New life in IKEA—just assemble.

—Matija Kalafatic

COMMUNIST HEALTH NUT,
HAMMER AND CYCLE.

—Brian John Evans

Should have lived more, written less.

—John Banville

"Give up."
  "Never."
    "You'll die."
      "Maybe."

—Jak Mandala

My son, forever 23, miss you.

—Colin Tierney

Ex-girlfriends
make the best
literary
material.

—Maya Stein

Smart girl wants love,
gets dog.

—Kathryn Horning

I've
done
it
all
except
hear.

—Marlee Matlin

I Google myself far too often.

—Marcus Eder

Ex-husband died. Forgave him too late.

—Erin Ruthven

My life, two words: fuck it.

—Henry Rollins

No longer youngest daughter. Youngest son.

—Adrien Arnao

PROSTATE HURTS
FROM ALL THE GRIEF.

—Gary Shteyngart

I should have killed her plant.

—Caitlin Kujawski

Came in shiny shoes,
left barefoot.

—Brian Salo

Unraveled career, reknitted as
baby blankets.

—Clare Hobba

Nice to many, available to few.

—Amelie A. Gagnon

Normal person becomes
psychotic on Twitter.

—Robin Slick

Full circle:
morgue tech becomes obstetrician.

—Andrea Skorenki

I turned eleven.
No Hogwarts letter.

—Laura Murray

Married three times.
Enjoyed all three.

—Chuck Taylor

Master of none; okay with that.

—Carmen McGee

Grandparents died
before I could ask.

—Nora Krug

Broke waitress. Gives tips. Is approved.

—Suze Orman

Was bored, went skydiving, now quadriplegic.

—Daniel Van Werkhoven

*Bimbo wannabe,
writer as second choice.*

—Isabel Allende

Can't reach top
shelves, married tall.

—Joy Zuercher

```
SWALLOWING PILLS,
THEY SWALLOWED ME BACK.
```

—Sarah Ladd

In a pickle? Not a problem.

—Rick Field

Been to five funerals, no weddings.

—Georgia Squyres

**Promised the moon,
dropped his pants.**

—Jeanette Cheezum

**Mom's Alzheimer's.
She forgets.
I remember.**

—Becky Blanton

Amazon woman.
Don't fuck with me.

—Camryn Manheim

Only if I can be naked.

—Gabriel Carleton-Barnes

Shirt:
Souvenir

Shoes:
Walmart

Soul:
PRADA.

—Astrid Muller

Living with balance, beauty, and inspiration.

—Eduardo Xol

Stricter parents could have saved me.

—David Macmillan Russell

We would have named him Xavier.

—Jose A. Amayo

Living my fourth draft. Revising regularly.

—Jeffrey Cufaude

I hated *Catcher in the Rye.*

—Amber Flood

Writing the next Great Albanian Novel.

—Nicole Hellene

Having "senior moments" at age 28.

—Kimber Jones

Son of psychopath, survived EuroDisney. Twice.

—Andrew Hall

Smithers's loyalty, Marge's probity, Lisa's perspicacity.

—A. G. Gordon

Said I walked into wall. Lied.

—Julianne Pepitone

The miserable childhood leads to royalties.

—Frank McCourt

Former zealot lost faith.
Tried bisexuality.

—M. A. Tyler

Quiet girl, big glasses, empty
stare.

—Leigh Spivey

Grew wings. Returning to my roots.

—Dana Newsome

I DON'T THINK I HAVE TIME.

—Margaret Cho

My father doesn't know I exist.

—Rebekah Young

I've moved but can't forget Miami.

—Noemy Sanchez

Family history: suicide. Personal history: perseverance.

—Breanne Derby

I threw a shoe at you.

—Greg Osisek

No reason to use good china.

—Laurie Schmidt

Late bloomer grows double D's. Whew!

—Gillian Zoe Segal

Brother's f'd-up exit: Booze. Gasoline.
Matches.

—Teri Porter

The Bobbsey Twins saved my life.

—Diane O'Neill

One-trick pony. One-horse cowboy.

—Christopher Wallace

Professional amateur, freelance loafer,
self-loathing narcissist.

—Zachary Riegle

Friends all pregnant, boyfriend fixed . . .
Fuck.

—Heather Kelsey

The
only
kid
unhappy
at
Disneyland.

—Daniel Coogan

He knew about her peanut allergy.

—Saaleha Bamjee-Mayet

I never got my blue bike.

—Dalia Grad

Cluttered. Christianity helps realign my disarray.

—Dayna Masih

Writer by night, critic by morning.

—Bethany Dale

Rape: herpes, pregnant, abortion. Thanks, asshole.

—Annie Evans

Septuagenarian athlete
regrets youth wasted writing.

—Jack Heinz

I'm finally out of the closet.

—Jessica Ensminger

Dancing naked
in my empty nest.

—Tammy Raye Wilson

Foot in grave, other in mouth.

—Bennett Ellenbogen

VONNEGUT HELPED KEEP ME
SANE. USUALLY.

—Mia Lipsit

For future reference, start Propecia earlier.

—Adam Roth

MOM: "JEWISH BOYS DON'T PLAY FOOTBALL."

—Michael Areinoff

Age twenty-three, scored pallbearer hat trick.

—Edward Doerr

Always "good friend," never girlfriend. Weary.

—Katherine Pease

Notebook missing; ideas come, then go.

—Leticia Britos-Cavagnaro

Age creeps up on your mirror.

—Valerie Ryan

Gets up early but blooms late.

—Christa Laib

Wanted warrior poet; got portfolio administrator.

—Sarah Serdin

Wife away, pizza today, diet tomorrow.

—David Logan

Two bad marriages. One excellent daughter.

—Dena Pruitt

Ancestors went steerage. I take subway.

—Maria Carmicino

I'm from Flint. You are, too.

—Michael Moore

At ten, had seven younger siblings.

—Shelby Grifo Swayze

Dating columnist.
Doesn't take own advice.

—Julia Allison

An obsessive-compulsive, bipolar, gender-dysphoric, social-phobic self-diagnoser.

—Kendra Thomas

Wanted love. Got lust. I'm screwed.

—Karen Taylor

Huh.
Hm.
Really?
Jesus!
Oy ve.

—Ian Sansom

Met wife at her bachelorette party.

-Eddie Matz

Muscles pushed the
            fat further out.

-Rudy Jaimes

*Airplane Bloody Mary diffuses
awaiting disappointments.*

-Natalie Shrock

I taped porn to your window.

-Heather Thomas

LEARNED MORE FROM POVERTY
THAN WEALTH.

-Michael Ragbourn

Web surfing. Coffee drinking.
Writer avoidance.

—Jan Bridgeford-Smith

Is beefcake one
word or two?

—James Worrall

If Raggedy Ann practiced poverty
law. . .

—Helene Busby

Learned protective coloration
earlier than most.

—Megan Porzio

Let me entertain you. No, please!

—Franz Nicolay

Black in America. And loving it.

—David Cummings

Was fat, now thin. Still unhappy.

—Nicole Hackenmiller

My mind danced, they suggested ADD.

—Brenna Reineck

I found God in a book.

—Alethea Black

```
Should have
revised that
middle chapter.
```

—Dan Kenney

One pregnancy, three kids.
All done!

—Tiffany Chesnosky

I found my mother's suicide note.

—Anne Heausler

Four days later, became single
mom.

—Julie Schuler

I have cleaned
all my life.

—Roger Ledford

Don't make me explain the
jokes.

—Mark Giles

Married Saturday. Left Sunday.
Reconsidered Monday.

—Caroline Robinson

I will sleep when I'm read.

—Rodes Fishburne

Please, Dad? It's only balsamic vinegar.

—Lindsay Champion

Dead bulimic sister, gay husband, me.

—Laurena Schultz

Running free. Running
wild. Running scared.

—Lia Moore

Michael Stipe mumbled my
formative years.

—Susan Haynes

Who? What? When?
Where? How? Why?

—Dyan Titchnell

Hotel sex still rocks over fifty.

—Marcella Oleksiuk

Fourth choice to prom. Still
overcompensating.

—Alisha Mckinney

Had my children, lost my identity.

—Christie Munro

*Thank you, Jonathan Larson, for
everything.*

—Kryss Shane

Confidence feigned, successes
gained, enthusiasm waned.

Elaine Grogan-Luttrull

Hopeless romantic finds
love between sheets.

—Sarah Morgan

Dicks are nice;
dykes are better.

—R. N. Brinegar

Left the typewriter on the curb.

—Kevin Evans

That Girl, enlightened, became
That Woman.

—Marlo Thomas

Miscarriage. Age 15. Mum doesn't
know.

—Nikki Stokes

Bow, arrows, pipe,
second-best pipe.

—Unwas Duwau

Found out my son isn't mine.

—Jonathan Sjørdal

A series of
self-fulfilling
prophecies.

—Jessie Rippel

I picked passion. Now I'm poor.

—Kathleen E. Whitlock

Cliché: met cop
at doughnut shop.

—Molly Hawley

Pants tight.
Comfort food.
Unending cycle.

—Elizabeth Catalano

—Dave Kiersh

One bodega. Three cousins.
Free cigarettes.

—Erica Ciccarone

*WASP, hippie, libber,
yuppie, techie,
boomer.*

—Sue Hamilton

Got your email today. Deleted it.

—Andrew Glaze

I am Muslim, not a
terrorist.

—Nur Amalina Khairul Anuar

Not fit for a real job.

—Will Peters

Thesis on cosmology; diploma typo:
cosmetology.

—Leila Belkora

Once in love, now in tears.

—Bethany Hicks

Parents are ministers.
I'm Gay. Boom!

—Steph Lee

25 years of "truthiness" ended Friday.

—Lisa Bottone

Curiosity killed cat. Eight lives left.

—Jennie Phillips

Art and opera keep me sane.

—Karen Coggeshall

Heroes: Dylan, Vonnegut,
Guthrie, King, Dad.

—Kate McNamara

My first addiction was to books.

—B. Chelsea Adams

These years writing
about those ones.

—Jamie-Lee Josselyn

One-night stand. Abortion.
Married. Infertile.

—Kathryn Cortelyou

I'm
so
tired
I'm
awake
again.

—Chelsea Handler

Three decades slathered in cat hair.

—Karla Keffer

Art, culture, technology, regurgitated by squid.

—Scott Beale

Woman mistakes job for a life.

—Betsy Rader

Wish I could bubble-wrap my son.

—Joellyn Bowser

I thought about God, so cool!

—Tommy Chong

Reading led to writing, days, years.

—Alan Cheuse

The recipricol vendettas never ended, unfortunately.

—Ben Bailey

Your practice made me forget "perfect."

—Tricia Callahan

Left behind; friends lost to marriage.

—James Littlejohn

Last chapter hasn't been written yet.

—Angie Stahl

It was always about the sex.

—Anna North

Peter Principle *and* Peter Pan Syndrome!

—Edward Kimble

Visted Kenya. Now building church there.

—Mary Wallace

He asked. It was about time.

—Lorraine Duffy Merkl

Why is it always about sex?

—Cole Kazdin

He's 26. I'm 40. Me cougar!

—Kelley Allison

Could not do, so I taught.

—Eric Viets

Mug shot was a flattering likeness.

—Timothy Miserendino

Life's good. *South Park* reminded me.

—Kei Black

One love, but many women friends.

—Dana Kelly

At
least
I
never
voted
Republican.

—Tony Kushner

Studied psych, went psycho,
searching psyche.

—Matt Lauterbach

"Don't settle."
"Yeah right."
And then . . .

—Craig Silverstein

Sentences got shorter. Suddenly became
novelist.

—Jessica Anthony

Fat feminist girl . . . famous, who knew?

—Kathy Najimy

Eye punctured; soul window forever
broken.

—Michelle Morales

—Alison Bechdel

Go green boho BAP. Urban debutante.

—Ananda Leeke

Happily married, until the paternity test.

—Terry Burlison

No dog, husband, kids; passport full.

—Laura Fraser

Resigned as the family's good girl.

—Erin Meyers

Manic-depressive without the lows— mostly.

—Diane Robitaille

Red neck, white trash, blue collar.

—Tracy L. Reeves

Quitting smoking
allowed me to feel.

—Cathy Bell

Looked up.
Saw sky.
Bird pooped.

—Robert Johnson

BADLY RAISED BY
BONKERS NAZI HIPPIE.

—Aubrey West

Class clown, class president, town
drunk.

—Victor Goad

Acting is not all I am.

—Molly Ringwald

Wedding dress stuffed into garbage can.

—Dan Campbell

`Mismatched dishes,`
`all of them dirty.`

—Leah Wiste

Read romances, met real man.
Disappointment.

—Melissa Allen

So I only get six words?

—Lalah Hathaway

Acted straight.
I deserve an Oscar.

—Jacob Devine

Newly converted conservative.
Still pro-choice feminist.

—Kellie Fournier

My work is another woman's
labor.

—Angie Miller

Birthed two. Adopted four.
Super mommy!

—Katie Holley

Geek gets LASIK,
life starts over.

—Liz Markman

Mommy,
why won't Daddy wake up?

—James DiGiovanna

Insomniac dreamer; a thousand times goodnight.

—Elisa Shevitz

Family portrait: everyone smiles but me.

—Ian Baaske

Welfare to academia.
Not that different.

—Erich Friedman

I rained on my own parade.

—Christopher J. Reiger

My life story—spay or neuter.

—Bob Barker

She became he.
Now gets Hemingway.

—Quince Mountain

Bought flowers and chocolate
for myself.

—Carole Inglis

Born 1971. ICWA became law 1978.

—Debbie Matson

Like Sudoku, my days are numbered.

—K. Dianne Thom

First math. Now writing.
What next?

—Jennifer 8 Lee

Failed teenage rebellion. Became school valedictorian.

—Jenn Yang

I wouldn't be me without OCD.

—Nadia Lahens

No kids, Internet date, step kids!

—Mike Lethem

Loves nature, works in a cube.

—Matthew Ford

We both reached for the gun.

—Ed Ramsell

Said vagina more
than necessary.
Vagina.

—Sarah Silverman

My love, his heart, their baby.

—Katherine Bedford

I felt a lump and laughed.

—Graham Peet

Wobbly feet, wobbly body, sharp mind.

—Adrienne Frances

Catholic school girl; future outspoken politician.

—Sara Maratta

I came, I saw, I worried.

—David Hirshey

I'm happiest when I'm eating cheesecake.

—Lindsey Rutherford

PROSECUTORS SUBMITTED
THE PACIFIER AS EVIDENCE.

—Roger Lee

I'm still mooching
off my parents.

—Jake Le Master

*Waiting for another
deus ex machina.*

—Rachel Turner

That college abortion
was very smart.

—Stephanie Losee

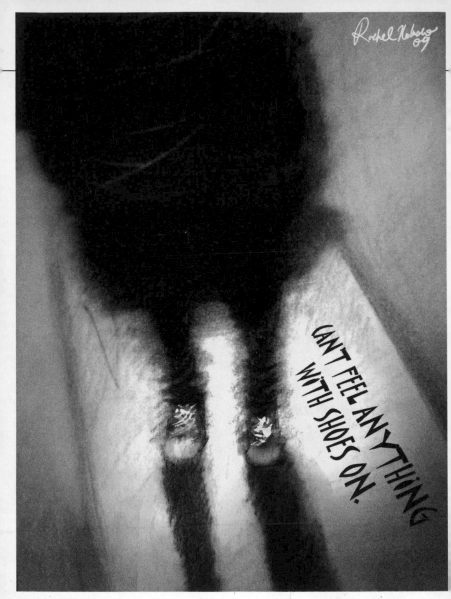

CAN'T FEEL ANYTHING WITH SHOES ON.

—Rachel Nolasco

Bright light. Drive toward it. Crash.

—Chelsea Tran

Meant to be a child star.

—Rob Williams

Went to shelter, found Amazing Gracie.

—Christie Bundy

Un peu fouillis. Pas encore compris.

—Ariane Eissen

Half-assed vegetarian:
I hate broccoli.

—Kathryn Kulpa

Blue-blood conservative caught
kissing crunchies.

—David Thompson

Dancing like
nobody can see,
finally.

—Sophia Bush

I want to be Tina Fey.

—Ellie McPherson

Overworked and underpaid,
Oversexed and underlaid.

—Victoria Hansen

I decided to leave the
bodies.

—Michael Hemmingson

Live man's life in woman's body.

—Diane von Furstenberg

Told to marry rich, married Richard.

—Jeaneen Morris

Little brother becomes my daughter's molester.

—Julie Taylor-Duncan

Little me would've liked big me.

—Tova Goodman

I inherited my Scottish great-grandmother's nose.

—Kaeli Grotz

My seizure disorder is still poetic.

—Casey Hannan

GROWN WOMAN, SLEEPS WITH
TEDDY BEAR.

—Karen Bates

I've sold my soul for peanuts.

—Eric Hamilton

Breast cancer: zero. My future: won.

—Amy Bowker

Five chambers full, pulled trigger once.

—Christian P. Dorko

Death knocked. I did not answer.

—Linda Farbstein

Shiny head.
Hippie hair.
Shiny head.

—Wally Lamb

Too much time spent on toilets.

—James Proctor

Blond hair, blue eyes, big
... brains.

—Annie Harris

Deaf parents taught me to sing.

—Lilit Marcus

The Fruit Loop among the Cheerios.

—Gabrielle Povolotsky

Now and always a mummy's boy.

—Alex Patterson

Never second guessed my own instincts.

—Shepard Fairey

Executive by day. Emcee by night.

—Jon DeLord

Loneliness: one egg in the pan.

—Penelope Vaillancourt

An adult collapses. A child cries.

—Joann Wang

Copyright 1945. Now out of print.

—James W. Beattie

Found Jesus, then somehow misplaced him.

—Robert Rowen-Herzog

Life is
one big
editorial
meeting.

–Gloria Steinem

Librarian, nurturer, knitter . . . still
a man.

—Karl G. Siewert

Rolled a few stones. Grew moss.

—Yvonne Ashmore

Wrong, Sartre: hell is panic disorder.

—Greta Boesel

He's not even worth five words.

—Heather Reddy

Parents Indian:
found tuna casserole
exotic.

—Madhu Dahiya

Create with passion,
publish with purpose.

—Brian Storm

Perfectionist loves her one crooked tooth.

—Mia Formichella

Becoming a rockstar to forget her.

—Jeremy Brockbank

```
Born, married, children,
grandchildren, divorced.
Happy!
```

—Ben Miyaji

I am losing 100 pounds again.

—Heather Lanham

Why is speaking true so courageous?

—Melissa Etheridge

Been around the block?
Only halfway.

—Heather Hannemann

Someone has to do the paperwork.

—Margie Gorman

Wanted steak,
stuck with beef jerky.

—Jessika Blanton

Clandestine fellatio, unrequited love,
jailbait fiasco . . .

—Winston Oberon Smith

Sonogram revealed twins.
Baby makes four!

—Felice Gold

"LOVE AND BE LOVED IN RETURN."

—Rick Parker

Little black sheep who's gone astray.

—Peter Renshaw

Connoisseur of coffee, wine, experience, mistakes.

—Annie Heintz

Law school trumps homosexuality, right Mom?

—Akhm Ouma

Started off normal, things went awry.

—Aurora Maxwell

Some are left alive, quick reload.

—Ann Coulter

Wish we were Elaine and Jerry.

—Elizabeth Dawe

`Won the`
`fellowship;`
`burned the`
`manuscript.`

—A. T. Lynne

Small girl dreams of heavyweight boxing.

—Lisa Johnson

Some days, "superwoman."
Other days, "nobody."

—Marianna Swallow

More sex than my looks deserve.

—Todd Zuniga

SCRAMBLING UP THE SCREE TOWARD ADULTHOOD.

—Kate Hamill

Got fired. Crazy, amazing, wonderful day.

—Kate Galbreath

Farm girl, city girl, farm girl.

—Tina Thomsen-Park

. . . and then the occasional good decision.

—Rob Erickson

Now, I know what you're thinking.

—The Amazing Kreskin

The inevitable triumph of the nerds.

—Craig Newmark

Tried, tried, tried, tried, tried . . . failed.

—Bob Odenkirk

I don't do Democrats or decaf.

—Lisa Baron

The Truth:
BUTTER MAKES EVERYTHING BETTER.

—Kelly Dixon

Turned lemons into lemonade. Added vodka.

—Leah Noble Davidson

Nordstrom prom date.
Thrift store dress.

—Jennifer Haggerty

MY DOGTAGS
DANGLE IN THE DIRT.

—Marcus Nogueira

Eschewed asceticism for
cheeseburgers, beer, sex.

—Tim Herbert

Here gay is the new black.

—Caprice Walker

Every day, a handful of pills.

—Danette C. Burchill

*My golden ticket was printed
incorrectly.*

—Lisa Marchal

With deep roots, branches soar skywards.

—Jonathan Blum

Just need three: work in progress.

—Emily Zemler

Oldest couple on the dance floor.

—Lee Anne Auerhan

Accidental math teacher loves skating, zombies.

—Megan Cleaver

I would pay retail for you.

—Lisa Rotenberg

Being nice. Having fun. Getting better.

—Andy Richter

Changed
sexes:
same
monkeys,
different
barrel.

—Jennifer Boylan

I thought you'd know my name.

—Naomi Major

Would prefer gay kids over vegetarians.

—David Yonan

Former drunken drummer,
now divorced dad.

—J. J. Doughty

I pick " . . . or the highway."
Bye!

—Genevieve Huot

I left a paper trail behind.

—Anne Burgot

Black? White? Best of both worlds.

—Scott Pierce

Eureka! Margin too small for proof.

—Marcus du Sautoy

That sounded better in my head.

—Nick Douglas

Birthmother found me through mom's obituary.

—Kate St. Vincent Vogl

Pole dancing classes equal newfound respect.

—Shannon Creekmur

I have Asperger's; what's your excuse?

—Ben Sheldon

Blond tramp found husband,
then conscience.

—Jamie Kasper

Trivial Pursuit helped
me find love.

—Heather S. Miceli

I think I survived almost everything.

—Sarah Manguso

Had kitties, not kiddies.
God misunderstood.

—Sue Burghard Brooks

We're both someone else's problem now.

—Litsa Dremousis

Off in my own little world.

—Aaron Renier

Pottstown. Princeton. Forever straddling two worlds.

—Sue Repko

Sought knight, now I need armor.

—Frauke Rona-Bowler

Husband. Kids. Park Slope. You know.

—Lori Leibovich

Got tattoo in basement, parents oblivious.

—Molly Savage

Final change to my Facebook status.

—Kim Mance

German-Jews. Dyslexia. Acting. Family.
Writing. Complete.

—Henry Winkler

Wanted a baby.
Got a miscarriage.

—Rhonda Parrish

42 faked 24,
went *Idol* audition!

—Ivan Chow

It all changed
in an instant.

—Candis Sykes

They called off the search
party.

—Bethany Browning

Emulated
Hemingway,
Bukowski;
just drunk now.

—Michael Gustie

My cat is an ungrateful brat.

—Nellie McKay

Jungle fever made his parents nervous.

—Allison Joseph

The world was enough. I wasn't.

—Michel Faber

Old scab still bleeds when picked.

—Pamela Walsh

Antique gardener, replanted, still dishes dirt.

—Marjorie Westphal

Josh ENJOYS Creating RICH MAGIC MOMENTS

—Josh McCutchen

As a toddler I ate tadpoles.

—Bob Shiffrar

Fortunate yet prepared.
Passionately driven.
Monkeyballs.

—Brian Baumgartner

Backstage is as drama-filled as on.

—Erin McIntosh

*The caterpillar became
a beautiful butterfly.*

—Kendall Hiedeman

*Desperate enough to read
my spam.*

—Caroline Braun

Adderall shriveled my dick and soul.

—Brendan Harrowby

So many sentences. Now this one.

—Mustafa Abdul-Wahid

CEO seeks inc.; no SEC, please.

—Jayati Jenkins

Analyst by training,
overanalyst by birth.

—Srinivasan Murali

*Couldn't say it,
so I sang.*

—Kenny Stapleton

That
dumb
dog
sure
paid
off.

—John Grogan

She left me for the librarian.

—Chris Clark

`Look how hard I rock, cocksuckers.`

—Charles Bock

Sixty: still haven't forgiven my parents.

—Russel Fershleiser

He got to meet his heroes.

—Jesse Thorn

Stole exit sign from wedding reception.

—Amy Hanson

So would you
believe me
anyway?

—James Frey

Supercomputer
in an Apple IIc world.

—Carrie Friedman

Accidentally, I'm 88 and still alive.

—Romualdo Binder

Author of so many unwritten books.

—Kirstin Pesola-McEachern

Jesus, hot hubby,
three awesome kids!

—Candace Cameron Bure

Honestly? I miss the eating
disorder.

—Danielle Cantor

There will be no white flag.

—Kamila Ema

She loves (I write). Her life.

—Miranda Seymour

Words unwisely chosen,
now doing better.

—Benny Green

I go with what I know.

—Jeffry Kerman

Spiritual,
uncanny
granny,
oversexed,
oversexed,
oversexed.

—Sylvia Bright-Green

Always the Dunkleman, never the Seacrest.

—Brian Marabello

Stop bothering me. Trying to work.

—Paul Whitehouse

Adventures, joys, love beyond my desserts.

—Max Hastings

I gave her the wrong flowers.

—Todd Austin Hunt

"Mommy," he told me, "is gone."

—Christine Lami

Don't know which
Self to synopsize.

—Art Spiegelman

Rose-tinted glasses
came in handy.

—Lee Payne

Saved the people
in my head.

—Hanna Utkin

Owning a bookstore.
Living the dream.

—Vicki Erwin

My sis caught me
wacking it.

—Richie Hume

Husband won heart. Babies stole it.

—Samantha Ettus

Philosophy student still
waiting for enlightenment.

—Hannah Stretton

The girl who took tobacco
down.

—Geraldine Lloyd

Waiting to awaken as a
cockroach.

—Hilary Bothma

Fired therapist. One mother is enough.

—Nina Spezzaferro

Yes, I still have Superman
sheets . . .

—M. C. Nicholson

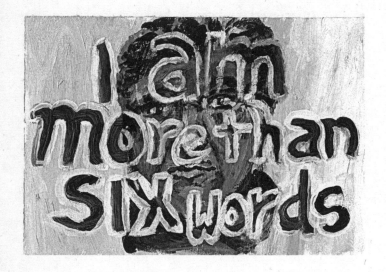

—J. Tony Smith

Blame Catholic church for
bad knees.

—Kathi Wright

Given two years,
going on sixth.

—Sheri Momaney

Happy we couldn't
conceive our own.

—K. C. Kirkpatrick

Learned how to bend, then broke.

—Troy Nickerson

North Dakota in my rearview mirror.

—Liz Cantarine

Brown skin invites judgement.
Bite me.

—Anita Victor

I stayed because
it was expected.

—Anthony Cortese

PostSecret saved my
sanity. Thanks, Frank.

—Sabrina Nevill

Book lover learns to
watch TV.

—Patti Thorn

Goth girl. White dog.
Lint roller.

—Megan Durham

Dad never
mentioned
drugs were
bad.

—Mackenzie Phillips

Sobriety died in my Champagne
flute.

—Nicole Haddow

Slept for at least two
words.

—Rodney Rothman

Most dying is done at
work.

—Cameron Vest

Everything I've made
can be deleted.

—Ben Brown

A nice Jewish girl singing gospel.

—Shari Salzhauer Berkowitz

Joined Rotary; beatnik parents mourn failure.

—Catharine Bramkamp

Wanted fewer husbands and more children.

—Jessica Anya Blau

Zigged when I should have zagged.

—Gary A. Forster

Even mad-eyed visionaries get the blues.

—Rebecca Brooks

Nobody ever sees me naked anyway.

—Phyllis Townsend

I aspire to capture the essence

—Rose Jaffe

Drunk husband's suicide still haunts me.

—Abbie Coppard

Wanted a pony, got a goldfish.

—Gretchen Cline

Eighties child, nineties teen, noughties statistic.

—Michael Beville

```
Vietnam Marine, got
shot, never forgot.
```

—Dennis M. Taylor

My next guest is Jesus Christ.

—Sir Michael Parkinson

Just white trash living middle class.

—Shane Faulkner

Single typist:
laugh 'til I cry.

—A. L. Kennedy

Two habitats. Cornwall.
Scotland. Lucky me.

—Rosamunde Pilcher

My little red dress;
partied out.

—Emily Maxine Gordon

Life is improv, marry a writer.

—Mark Feuerstein

I wish I had more words.

—Tyler Shores

Indonesian. Stanford. Fell for
Arkansas boy.

—Dian Rosanti

Found on Craigslist: table, apartment, fiancé.

—Becki Lee

Nephew's flip-flops clapping behind
me. Heaven!

—Tsia Harris

Wasn't really crazy, just needed insulin.

—Christy Allen

Never found religion,
always slept well.

—Jesse Silverstein

Started off kosher.
Then, discovered bacon.

—Anna Wexler

Traveled on TV,
world saw me.

—Vinnie Costa

Three terrible words:

Inoperable. Brain. Tumor.

—David L. Tamarin

Wrote SLUT on her dirty windshield.

—Katherine T. Paterson

I never checked my lottery ticket.

—Casey Burra

Father:
"Anything but
journalism."
I rebelled.

—Malcolm Gladwell

Went to college,
came home pregnant.

—Sharon Lorimor

Shhh, not now. Mama's writing smut.

—Kimberly J. Cockrill

Still awaiting *Twin Peaks'*
season three.

—Leigh Buchanan

Art therapist, more fun than doctor.

—Jackie Verrecchia

After cancer,
I became a semicolon.

—Anthony R. Cardno

Turned out exactly as parents predicted.

—C. M. Fields

Brezhnev, Reagan, Bush, Clinton, Bush, Obama.

—Elaine Shpungin

Danced in rain.
Caught pneumonia.
Danced.

—Stephanie Marcellin

Got drunk, called mom a cunt.

—Steve Coulter

Born from sperm on a finger.

—Julian Baker

Ideas wake me,

motherhood overtakes me . . .

—Amanda Joann Smith-Holtom

Met the geek of my dreams.

—Dana Eades

Sold Rolls-Royces. Had no choices.

—Linda Stromme

Size 14, size 16, size 18.

—Sue Knottenbelt

I LOVE MY BIG, BIG BALLS.

—Rob Riggle

My loonball
radar keeps
me sane.

—Anna Raff

Experienced reincarnation without bothering to die.

—Jerilyn Wissa

Ex-boyfriends' new girlfriends: model, heiress, chanteuse.

—Nicole Tourtelot

I already know how it ends.

—Bill McLaughlin

Hindu, Catholic . . . both agnostic . . . Who cares?

—Hanorah Slocum

I was born in a lighthouse.

—William Sinnott

I bribed my way into Russia.

—Jesse Chan-Norris

Thankfully, the snow
covered our tracks.

—Susan Friberg

Embarrassed to
love yoga this
much.

—Emily Zackin

Took breath. Took ill.
Took notes.

—Hilary Mantel

Three years,
eight surgeries,
still shattered.

—Bella Stander

Two said, "I do." One did.

—Larry McCann

College, DUI, AA.
The party ended.

—Sabrina Rivera

Fibromyalgia.
Polycystic ovarian
syndrome. Only sixteen.

—Leah Mitchell

Found bra in backseat. Not mine.

—Cari Kidd

Witness Protection
is not much fun.

—Joseph Sharp

Happiness is not becoming your parents.

—Norah Vincent

Eternal teenager trying for Donna Reed.

—Katie Donahue

Born a tone-deaf singer; color-blind painter.

—Katy Reinsel

Degree in English. I sell furniture.

—Jessica Leichsenring

Ending our relationship on Facebook? Classy.

—Quin Browne

Beat down. Locked up. Still standing.

—Adrian King

Let Go of The Last Straw

—Ema Chen

Checked luggage but skipped
baggage claim.

—Daniel Stasiewski

I'm in love with my cousin.

—Elsie Lopez

Missed subway stop.
Like this better.

—Mark Rosenblum

I've had Access to a lot.

—Nancy O'Dell

I have finally learned cliffhangers are

—Caitlin O'Connor

Daughter, wife, mother,
divorcée, widow, "Gama."

—Kathleen Faraday

She died. Found her
diary. Wow.

—Amanda La Valley

Went abroad gray; came back
magenta.

—Lindsay Galan

Found myself
but lost my hair.

—David Thorpe

Ride the bull, live in
technicolor.

—Tovah Feldshuh

Love and marriage.
Death and taxes.

—Ann Heiney

Day not complete
without crossword puzzle.

—Christine Junge

Herpes? Really? You're
fucking kidding me.

—Ashley D'Amore

Writer quits day job. Send food.

—Kimberly T. Thompson

I am one of
Jehovah's Witnesses.

—Zenovia Barksdale

I
have
to
constantly
reinvent
myself.

—Terry McMillan

Optimistic pessimist. Introverted extrovert.
Realistic extremist.

—Dayna Goldberg

Could be poop, could be chocolate.

—Erin Kennedy

Old age is not all bad.

—Anna Massey

Tried atheism once; still loved God.

—Ariel Rivas

Poor immigrant: changed
countries like underwear.

—Mark Budman

About three inches short of pleasure.

—Chanel Merlise Sutherland

Never could save.
Money or myself.

—Eric Bakkum

25, been seeing
shrink since 15.

—Abiy Wright

Lesbians always
mistake me for one.

—Tommy Wong

Two wrongs don't;
three lefts do.

—David N. James

Work in suit, play in underwear.

—Toni Giarnese

Fell in love with nomad.
Moved.

—Janice Lewis

Ten years old, combed
hair twice.

—Noah Michaud

SLOW LEARNER: LIFE
BEGAN AT FIFTY.

—Arnold Simon

Redhead, need I
say more?

—Susan Orlean

Affair with philosophy professor was transcendental.

—Susan Breeden

Relying on serendipity since September 1980.

—Art Kelly

Math geek prefers cooking to calculus.

—Michele Richardson

And then I started getting paranoid.

—Alex Scala

Rockin', geekin', oversexed whimsical faerie boy.

—Jason Willis

Lost everything but my loving husband.

—Anne Sexton

Steroid use, a hollow fame career.

—Martin Hemerik

Alone, since they cut the
cord.

—Ashley Kjos

Love NBA, 52 inches, must wait.

—J. J. Randazzo

Visited London
in 1977.
Changed plans.

—John Flansburgh

—Ted Rall

Inquisitive, excited, surprised, and
sometimes wrong.

—Jon Snow

Good housekeeper.
I got the house.

—Nancy McPeak

Aimed for moon. Lost in space.

—Anthony Grant Gordon

God, no God. Job, no job . . .

—Charles Wright

People like the books I like.

—Eric Simonoff

Pickles, pregnancy, puking, pain,
premature. Priceless.

—Sherry Rentschler

Met online. Got married. Internet rocks.

—Judy Chang

Cripple saved. Hips replaced at 14.

—Holly Hoar

Thousands of aquaintances.
Very few friends.

—Savannah Ganster

Woke up,
stepped in pee again.

—Heather Moran-Botta

Jewish dad, Wiccan mom, so fucked.

—Ashlea Halpern

Characters leapt seductively
off my pages.

—David Brennan

My parents took
away my child.

—Samantha M. Pendleton

Quarter-life. Lost.
Found in a keg.

—Michelle Winslow

Busy missing
opportunties or
dodging bullets.

—Todd Rosenberg

Pivotal discoveries: clitoris, Internet, gin, you.

—Kate Beall

I make comic books, not friends.

—A. Daniel Curtindolph

Writer explores truths about father's murder.

—Rita Schiano

Counts days in birth control pills.

—Sarah Faraji

Got bangs, they're cheaper than Botox.

—Wendy West Hickey

Yoga, meditation, workouts, art. 75. Strong.

—Bee Colman

Here's my secret: location, location, relocation.

—Gord Sellar

Hated seventh grade. Now teaching it.

—Tara Morrison

My life is a to-do pile.

—Keith Herrmann

Buried my brother on my birthday.

—Chris Rigakos

Red wine and Internet. Marriage doomed.

—Kathleen Nalley

Dad died.
Mum died.
I'm next.

Jim Crace

Mom's dead.
Dad's dead.
I'm free.

—Barbara Gordon

I spent Christmas alone. At 10.

—Qraig deGroot

Found my calling by
flunking out.

—Daphne Tobin

Hitler and Jews;
Mom and me.

—Jak King

Fun in the sun. Then
jail.

—James Cohen

"Live long and
prosper" says it.

—Leonard Nimoy

—Lisa Anne Auerbach

Virgin 'til 23, total slut after.

—Suzanne Siegel

Heart in SF, arm in Vietnam.

—Harlan Stanton

I ran with scissors and lived.

—Rienne Smith

```
I cross-stitch, therefore
I am.
```

—Justine MacDonald

Dream big. Work hard. Work hard.

—Perez Hilton

I have stopped recognizing my reflection.

—Jillian Boshart

No one reads my online journal.

—Anna Edlund

Saturday evening. Internet. I have friends.

—Nikhil Gupta

They don't know I know Spanish.

—Lisa Davis

College: zombie hunting, NERF guns, bruises.

—Bailey Shoemaker Richards

Unexpectedly,
    However belatedly,
        Love came gracefully.

—C. C. Keiser

Lost at love. Won at Scrabble.

—Kyle Zukauskas

Part time writer.
Full time waitress.

—Erin Hicks

Learning to save money saved me.

—Allison Cote

Dad twice; husband once; myself zero.

—Joe Webster

Barney . . . Doogie . . !
Average names elude me.

—Neil Patrick Harris

Too bad, such a pretty face.

—Ali Waks

. . . but then he told me no.

—Krissy Houston

I found myself living jungle life.

—Andrea Wady

Married three times,
divorced three times.

—Dave Lopez

The only way out is in.

—Junot Díaz

A million souls, I was alone.

—Joseph Arthur

Lost girl, always carries a pen.

—Amanda Paweska

Married longer than single. Slightly sad.

—Angela Smith

Retired: one errand takes all day.

—Bobbie Slonevsky

Bring a date to my shiva.

—Steven Liss

My blog is banned in China.

—Sandra Hanks Benoiton

Was a painting, now a mural.

—Charlie Newman-Johnson

Shocked the masses.
Kicked their asses.

—Lisa Lampanelli

Lived a dream riding a skateboard.

—Tony Hawk

Tried to say yes to everything.

—Amanda Weldin

Took much acid. Slowly coming to.

—Nate Beaty

Girl inside the woman wants out.

—Elissa Schappel

Head often buried in census records.

—Gabrielle Adams

He left. Sparked my personal D-Day.

—Beth Carter

Marissa, Erika, Sarah: beginning, middle, end.

—Chris Shaw

This was for a homework assignment.

—Shandiin Woodward

Cynical optimist: never surprised,
always disappointed.

—Felicia Ramsey

Called Dad asshole. Lost left eye.

—George Rosa

Actor, goth, bibliophile, mother, nerd,
otaku.

—Stephanie Howard

Lost four toes, can still mambo.

—Roxanne Hoffman

I miss fitting in the Batmobile.

—Forrest Gaddis

God,
how
long
was
I
asleep?

—Christopher Rumsey

Redwoods married desert.
California cradles me.

—Amanda Jordan

I masturbate three times a day.

—Tim Wilson

Ordered victory, got served
humble pie.

—John Sampson

Teen war-bride waiting by the mailbox.

—Jacqueline Goodrich

"Too many sermons!" the pastor
proclaimed.

—Will Humes

The only orange lacking in vitamins.

—Michelle Orange

Trivia-night hero. Work place zero.

—Joseph P. Molinari

Bipolar, no two ways about it.

—Jason Owen

Married young. Discovered dating
soon after.

—Jill Mancini

Almost twenty-one and never
been kissed.

—Avery Canapini

Can't
look
at
heart
donor's
picture.

—Tonia Hall

And she lived happily ever after.

—Poppy Montgomery

Hippie met redneck, opposites horribly attracted!

—Emily Dorney

Like a ring without a finger.

—Matt Gallo

My life:
I Love Lucy episode.

—Patti Williams

Hm.
Are we nearly there
yet?

—DBC Pierre

Womb. Bloom. Groom.
Gloom. Rheum. Tomb.

—Blake Morrison

Failed relationships. Donor sperm.
    With child.

—Robin Beers

Kindergarten teacher sent to
insane asylum.

—Samantha Fillian

Novels and sunshine and
strawberry smoothies.

—Laurel Rhame

Love at first sight.
Needed glasses.

—Susan Holcombe

Started with shots, ended without clothing.

—Rachel Levine

Twenty toes, four countries, three daughters.

—Katrin Talbot

I still practice my Oscar speech.

—Jennifer Labbienti

Laying the flowers down, he wept.

—Paolo Vaglietti

I have even Twittered during sex.

—John M. Quick

—Caty Bartholomew

My alpaca died. We ate her.

—James Kellar

Writing teen novels.
The angst lives.

—Melissa Walker

I like hiding
in plain sight.

—Nicole Salzano

Steve McQueen,
Chuck Yeager,
Julia Child.

—Duff Goldman

Different grass.
Same shade of green.

—Julia Schofield

Fucked up. Sobered up. Growing up.

—Brad Hood

Me: faithful scientist. Her:
new-age philanderer.

—David Rhodes

Church bells and coffee.
Perfect Sunday.

—James Reilly

**Alzheimer's:
meeting new people
every day.**

—Phil Skversky

Eat. Bloat. Fingers
down throat.
Shame.

—Donna Murphy-Lelie

Story of my life? Bad timing.

—Brooke Marie Gorman

Yale at 16, downhill from there.

—Anita Kawatra

Life's a tux.
I'm brown shoes.

—Jimmy Aquino

Should have crossed legs,
not fingers.

—Sharon Faltisek

I love me some me,
dammit!

—Terrell Owens

Healed with steel, then got real.

—Dr. Mehmet Oz

Ruby's slippers won't take her home.

—Ruby Andrews

Spent money on shoes and handbags.

—Julie Benz

Dad died. Nobody called me. Oops.

—Marcia Evers

Family: priority. TV: obsession. Surfing: passion.

—Alexander Sawicki

Neurotic hypochondriac seeks medical attention, please.

—Jessica Lester

I love to read
celebrity smut!

—Nadia Garnett

Dad got promoted. I miss him.

—Ana Maria Uribe

Always torn between roots and
wings.

—Staeven Lewis Frey

Evangelicals scared bejesus out of me.

—Caitlyn Paley

Nine years stacked
within my soul.

—Laura Sussman

Journalism? Hah! Just make stuff up.

—Dave Barry

Auschwitz child.
American citizen:
Thanks, America!

—Annalie Nossbaum

Working same job as my grandpa.

—Jeanmarie Riquelme

Always last to get the joke.

—Chantal Braganza

Sadly, we have registered at Goodwill.

—Gary Houy

Hopelessly idealistic.
Call me Donna Quixote.

—Erin Rickard

Opinionated: Cupcakes–good.
Jam bands–bad.

—Katty Biscone

Always searching for the
right level.

—Michael Morrison

Small fish. Big pond.
All sharks.

—Audrey Adu-Appiah

I'm forever painting myself
painting myself.

—Corey Ginsberg

I can't proffread my own writing.

—Amy M. Litt

Texas cheerleader writes recipe for revolution.

—Frances Moore Lappé

Berkeley foodie to
Brooklyn baby's boobie.

—Anna Lappé

Exposing hypocrites, trying not to be one.

—Anthony Lappé

Met and married in two months.

—Stacey Nerdin

They always tell me to smile.

—Emily Farris

Don't speak Greek. Didn't speak English.

—Judson Morrow

Gay rehab doesn't work at all.

—Weston Ashley

Practice every day, you get better.

—Kenny G

Hit me, I'll hit you back.

—Mark Zupan

My life popped like a zit.

—Lauren Rosen

Machetes, revenge, and butterflies reflect Congo.

—Brian Wood-Koiwa

Navy brat: ship without an anchor.

—Amy Miller

I'm vegan, but I kill spiders.

—Alison Carey

I secretly liked my debutante ball.

—Kate McNeil

Planted a garden and
smoked weed.

—Matthew Schmeer

Same crimes, different people,
usual suspects.

—Heather Clark

24,900 Google hits on my name.

—Alessandra Rizzotti

I fake everything except the orgasms.

—Tammy Everts

Photo by Kathleen Johnstone

Saved from pound, killed by opossum.

—Mary Ellen Mark

Struggling with secret, weary,
still hiding.

—Danny Bates

Ms. Smith before, Ms. Smith again.

—Marilyn Smith

Oxford English applicant,
favourite literature: erotica.

—J. S. Hamilton

Think hard. Work smart. Play often.

—Timothy Ferriss

Dealt better with rejection than success . . .

—Rick Mele

Moved to Mexico old, awoke young.

—Joanne Howard

Laughed all the way ... bank's closed.

—Brendon Cassezza

I got dumped for a skateboard.

—Maggie Adams

Felled by tyranny
of the newspeg.

—Mikki Halpin

At 96 still
use my dick.

—Franz Brandenberg

Quiet baby who nuzzled Mom's breast.

—Phillip Lopate

Heard some Shakespeare. Never went back.

—Casey O'Toole

Blissfully surviving
a perpetually broken heart.

—Maija Meadows

Insulin. Marijuana.
My drugs of choice.

—David Setzler

No thumb (amputee). Still gives
handshakes.

—Kendall Jordan Humbert

Named plain on purpose. Didn't work.

—Ayun Halliday

Viewed life from behind a camera.

—Kimberly Pfirrmann-Powell

Exhausted writer flees on lovely rocketship.

—Jason Boog

He taught me; he married me.

—Lenore Balliro

A shining example of Detroit's East Side.

—Vin Dombroski

Skinny. Cancer. Skinnier. Cured. Famous. Fat.

—Evan Handler

Just some schlub who cures kids.

—Sri Narayanan

Married at 18. Remarried at 30.

—Jamee T. Perkins

Beer, pizza. Who needs six words?

—Ron Heller

Dealt bad cards. Played them well.

—Joe Queenan

I'm a visual thinker—understand animals.

—Dr. Temple Grandin

Eat, Pray, Love changed my life.

—Trish Smith

Ate, prayed, and loved, but differently.

—Andy Raskin

I lost, but I never cheated.

—Joshua Pitkoff

Regularly disqualifying myself for public office.

—Jess Walter

Unknown author today, enduring author tomorrow.

—David Clary

weirdo finds happiness with other weirdos

—Anya Davidson

Rotten uterus, poisoned ovaries,
21, infertile.

—Charn Taylor

Not enough Wellbutrin in the
world.

—Steve Kovach

Little boy,
now a dad. Oy!

—David Wain

Found tumor. Removed kidney.
Turned four.

—Shayna Bauchner

Am sometimes mistaken for a prostitute.

—Jennifer Companik

I'm holding on with both hands.

—Denise Moore

Katrina was not a nice lady.

—Brobson Lutz

Fighting fire with fire does
nothing.

—Kwame Webster

Never did have anything to say.

—Michelle Alcina

Meanwhile, back home in New Orleans . . .

—Leo McGovern

It ain't over 'til it's over.

—Yogi Berra

Grandpa's a tough act to follow.

—Lindsay Berra

Border guards never remember
my name.

—Charles London

I could never get anything quite right.

—Harry Enfield

Habitual mind changer . . .
wait, scratch that.

—Erica Dolinky

Heart fattens, skin thins.
Who knew?

—Sloane Crosley

I feel like a jelly bean.

—Debra Goodman Benson

My teeth hurt.
Who hit me?

—Shelley White

Books then. Books now. Occasionally life.

—Nancy Pearl

Earth was definitely
my second choice.

—R. Steven Renfro

After ages, I met my dad.

—Bryony-Lee Penn

Finding myself by process of elimination.

—Jonathan Stefiuk

—Adriano

Too good to be true. Sociopath.

—Liliana Frieiro

One plane ride can change everything.

—Mei-Ling Hopgood

I live with feelings of regret.

—Said Sayrafiezadeh

Never lacks drama, yet seeks peace.

—Jessica Queller

I forgot my six-word memoir.

—Lizzy Charnas

Six words not
enough for a

—Laura Hillenbrand

Screw diabetes, pass me another cookie.

—Louis Smith

Job advancement, penis,
both in downturn.

—Steve Straight

Say when, childhood whispered, pouring,
spilling.

—JR Moehringer

Stillness is timeless dancing happening
now.

—Rodney Yee

For Sale: Adult shoes.
Never worn.

—Jonathan Coulton

Horrible with deadlines, even this one.

—Starlee Kine

The songs are in the shadows.

—Pepi Ginsberg

Back in junior high, *nobody* laughed.

—Peter Sagal

Disarm them by seeming sorta nice.

—Naomi Klein

Across the street, the generations repeat.

—Carol Smith

Shy megalomaniac, willing to be lucky.

—Kurt Anderson

Rheumatoid arthritis determines my day's productivity.

—JarieLyn Robbins

A story told with every wrinkle.

—Beth Canton

Rescued dog, saved self, world next.

—Deanna Zandt

I've fucked at least eight people.

—Eugene Mirman

My six words haven't happened yet.

—Erica Ray

I was never one for pith.

—Ethan Hiedeman

The main thing is I laughed.

—Bryan Butler

It was all too brief.

—Rudolph Delson

Am hoping there is an epilogue.

—Margot Beverley

Selected Bios, Backstories, Correspondence, and Conversations
with Six-Word Memoirists Famous & Obscure

Lisa Anne Auerbach ("Everything I touch turns to mold," p. 177) is an artist living in Los Angeles. In addition to taking photographs and preparing small-batch publications, she makes sweaters, including the one you see pictured with her six words. "I've been obsessed with sweaters for quite a while," she says. "I like when the knitted slogans wear out much more quickly than the fabric." On the back of the pictured sweater are the following words: "Steal this sweater off my back, free to a good home."

Bob Barker ("My life story—spay or neuter," p. 84) was the host of *The Price is Right* for thirty-five years and in 1979 became a noted animal activist and vocal vegetarian.

Alison Bechdel ("Drawing . . . Writing . . . Running out of material," p. 78) is the author of the graphic memoir *Fun Home,* a finalist for the 2006 National Book Critics Circle Award, and creator of the comic strip *Dykes to Watch Out For.* When contacted she said, "I didn't register that there was an actual Smith behind SMITH. I thought it was just a cool name."

Debra Goodman Benson ("I feel like a jelly bean," p. 221) is a zookeeper and a mother of two teenage boys ("same thing, really") living in Tucson, Arizona. About her memoir, she says, "It comes from a saying my grandmother used when she felt her heart would burst with joy. So it's a tribute to her, a flamboyant character who died before I could truly appreciate her. And now I annoy my kids with it. I think it totally captures some moments."

Andy Borowitz ("Born with big nose. Pursued comedy," p. 25) is the creator of the Web site Borowitz Report (borowitzreport.com), an author, stand-up comedian, and the first-ever recipient of the National Press Club Award for being funny. When solicited for a six-word memoir via Facebook, he responded in approximately ninety seconds—so we know he writes his own stuff.

Candace Cameron Bure ("Jesus, hot hubby, three awesome kids!" p. 130) is an actor best known for playing D. J. Tanner on the popular sitcom *Full House*.

Ann Coulter ("Some are left alive, quick reload," p. 106) is a political pundit and bestselling author, most recently of *Guilty: Liberal "Victims" and Their Assault on America*. She submitted her six-word memoir around the time we were completing our previous book, *Six-Word Memoirs on Love and Heartbreak*, and made sure that we were straight on the fact that her "memoir is not about love."

Susan Cushman ("The upside of Alzheimer's: 'new' mother," p. 7) is a writer living in Memphis, Tennessee, where she is working on a full-length memoir. About her six words, she says, "My mother is eighty-one. The good news about her Alzheimer's is that she has almost quit putting me and everyone else down all the time. Maybe the disease has killed her judgmental self and left a sweeter mom in its place. It is what it is."

Unwas Duwau ("Bow, arrows, pipe, second-best pipe," p. 65) is an elder in the Hadza tribe of northern Tanzania, one of the last hunter-gatherer groups on earth. This memoir has been translated from the Hadzane, thought to be one of the oldest languages still in existence. In the rather lengthy translation session this memoir required, Unwas interpreted "six-word memoir" to mean "the most important words to him"—which were, in turn, the most important objects to him.

Timothy Ferriss ("Think hard. Work smart. Play often," p. 210) is the author of *The 4-Hour Workweek:*

Escape 9–5, Live Anywhere, and Join the New Rich, which hit the number-one spot on both the *Wall Street Journal* and *New York Times* bestseller lists.

John Flansburgh ("Visited London in 1977. Changed plans," p. 167) is an actor, musician, and member of the Grammy Award–winning rock band They Might Be Giants. He's also directed music videos for Soul Coughing and Ben Folds Five, starred in the off-Broadway musical *People Are Wrong!*, and describes himself as "manic depressive, without the depression."

Duff Goldman ("Steve McQueen, Chuck Yeager, Julia Child," p. 167) is the owner of the Baltimore-based custom cake shop Charm City Cakes and the star of Food Network TV show *Ace of Cakes*.

John Grogan ("That dumb dog sure paid off," p. 127) is the author of the canine memoir, *Marley & Me*, which has nearly six million copies in print, and was made into a film starring Owen Wilson and Jennifer Aniston.

Chelsea Hadley ("Learned to draw with my foot," p. 6) is Director of Major Gifts at the Los Angeles County Museum of Art and a sometime portraitist who uses photography, paint, and black Sharpies. As with the self-portrait that accompanies her memoir, she occasionally draws with a pen held between her prehensile toes.

Anita Hahn ("Sent home. Baby born in bathtub," p. 8) lives in Delta, Utah, with her husband of thirty-five years. About her memoir, she says, "I drove myself to the hospital. It took twenty minutes to get the four miles because I had to stop every five minutes to breathe through each contraction. When I got there at 2 A.M., the aging doctor was not happy to have been awakened and told the nurse over the phone that he wouldn't induce. He ordered a sedative and told me to go home. I was naïve enough to believe they knew what they were talking about. Crying, I called my husband at the power plant he ran and told him to please come home; then I climbed into the bathtub, concentrated on the hot-water stream on my belly, and cried more. After the hot water ran out, I felt the urge to push. And there she was. Now she is thirty."

Evan Handler ("Skinny. Cancer. Skinnier. Cured. Famous. Fat," p. 214) is a leukemia survivor, author, and actor who, most famously, played Harry Goldenblatt on *Sex and The City.*

Anne Heausler ("I found my mother's suicide note," p. 60) was born in New Orleans, and has spent the past thirty years in New York City's Hell's Kitchen, where she acts, edits, and volunteers with kids. About her memoir, she says, "When I was thirteen, my mother killed herself after suffering with lifelong depression. It was the sixties and the South, and my father couldn't admit it was suicide, even after I showed him the note. Though I wasn't told the truth, having found her note was liberating and confirmed that I knew what had happened. The note was six words: 'No funeral, no wake, no nothing.'"

Taylor Hicks ("From bar singer to Halloween costume," p. 27) was born in Birmingham, Alabama, in 1976 and won the fifth season of *American Idol* in 2006.

Phil Jacobsen ("Peed on White House floor. Really," p. 2) is a mailman in Salt Lake City. About his memoir, he says, "I was on a private tour of the White House when I saw a nondescript door where real presidential business took place. A bathroom. At this moment I knew I could do in the White House what dignitaries, chancellors and even Elvis had possibly done. I could do Number One at 1600 Pennsylvania Avenue. The tour guide said, 'no' when I asked for relief, but at that moment this word was not part of my vocabulary. I stepped in, closed the door and reached out my arms touching both walls. A bathroom slightly larger than an upright coffin had seen some of the most influential members in history. And now, mine too. It wasn't just relief I wanted; I needed to leave my mark. I took aim and then turned to the left. Really."

Naomi Klein ("Disarm them by seeming sorta nice," p. 227) is the internationally bestselling author of *The Shock Doctrine: The Rise of Disaster Capitalism.*

The Amazing Kreskin ("Now, I know what you're thinking," p. 108) has been called the "Nostradamus of the twentieth century" and is arguably the world's foremost mentalist. He's had a TV show, board game, written sixteen books, and appeared on nearly every talk show in the United States.

Nora Krug ("Grandparents died before I could ask," p. 38) is a thirty-two-year-old illustrator living in New York City. About her memoir, she says, "Germans of my generation grew up with a deep feeling of guilt and shame. From early on, I learned in detail about what happened in my country before my parents were born. When traveling abroad as a teenager, I felt awkward letting people know I'm German. Sometimes I was greeted with *'Heil Hitler'* in response. Even though I know that my grandparents weren't direct supporters of the National Socialists, I never was able to find out what they really thought and did, or rather, didn't do. I was a child when they died; they never talked about the war to my parents."

Tony Kushner ("At least I never voted Republican," p. 76) is an essayist, a screenwriter, and the Pulitzer Prize–winning playwright of *Angels in America.* He submitted this six-word memoir prior to the 2008 election.

Amanda La Valley ("She died. Found her diary. Wow," p. 160) is a recent graduate of Brighton High School in Brighton, Colorado, a small town about twenty minutes north of Denver. She found the diary mentioned in her memoir in the summer of 2008, in a nursing home in Lakewood, Colorado, after her great-grandmother passed away. Here's an excerpt from the diary. "March 14, 1984. I like things that look small from far away but are actually big up close, like a car or a button. I wanted to be a poet, and every day I regret becoming a nurse. But I still write poetry. Are you a poet if nobody reads your poems? I read them. The sunlight reads them. Maybe some day someone else will read them. I almost ripped the pages out and buried them so they'd be forever mine. I almost burned them into the earth. I was angry. I wanted to destroy. I was out for blood poems. If even one person read this, I'll be satisfied with my job as a nurse. Deep down, I know I am a poet."

Neil LaBute ("Writing is easy. Life is hard," p. 1) is an author and the playwright of *In The Company of Men* and, most recently, *reasons to be pretty*, which features a *Playbill* author note containing the above six words. In addition to granting permission to print those words as his six-word memoir, he has also submitted, "I loved her once. Forgive me," on SMITHmag.net.

Geraldine Lloyd ("The girl who took tobacco down," p. 135) is an artist and writer living in Frederick, Maryland. About her memoir, she says, "My great-grandfather, John W. Lucas, a century ago, with a cigarette between his lips, said to James Buchanan Duke, the tobacco magnate, 'I'd walk a mile for a Camel.' Three generations of tobacco addiction, cancer, death, and mutilation resulted in the removal of my voice box in 1995. It spurred a fourteen-year relentless personal activism that gained momentum and was able to influence the passage of the Family Prevention and Smoking Control Act, finally giving the FDA authority to regulate tobacco. My story was read before the Senate on June 2, 2009."

Brobson Lutz ("Katrina was not a nice lady," p. 219); **Denise Moore** ("I'm holding on with both hands," p. 219); **Kwame Webster** ("Fighting fire with fire does nothing," p. 219); **Leo McGovern** ("Meanwhile, back home in New Orleans . . . " p. 219); and **Michelle Alcina** ("Never did have anything to say," p. 219) are former and current residents of New Orleans. They are all featured in the nonfiction graphic novel *A.D.: New Orleans After the Deluge* by Josh Neufeld.

Debbie Matson ("Born 1971. ICWA became law 1978," p. 85), thirty-eight years old, lives in Vermillion, South Dakota, and is about to start her first year of law school. About her memoir, she says, "I was born in Anchorage, Alaska, in 1971. My mother was fifteen years old when she gave birth to me and could not care for me. My adoptive, 'white' parents were hoping to adopt a baby girl. I am an Alaskan native, from the Athabascan tribe. ICWA, the Indian Child Welfare Act, was designed to protect the best interest of Native American children and their families and to help preserve Native American culture. My tribe is very poor and I do not feel that I would have as many opportunities or resources had I been forced to stay within my tribe."

Frank McCourt ("The miserable childhood leads to royalties," p. 44) was a school teacher and author of three memoirs, including *Angela's Ashes*. When McCourt first submitted his six words, via e-mail, the editors realized it was only five words. In response to our panicked reply, McCourt graciously offered: "I thought I'd get away with it. 'Brevity is the soul of wit,' said that English bard."

And then he added a sixth word. A few months later, he passed away on July 19, 2009.

Noah Michaud ("Ten years old, combed hair twice," p. 165) and **Laura Sussman** ("Nine years stacked within my soul," p. 201) hail from Moorestown, New Jersey. Shortly after the release of *Not Quite What I Was Planning: Six-Word Memoirs by Writers Famous and Obscure,* Noah invited SMITH Magazine editors to come speak to his third-grade class, where they talked about the power of personal storytelling and then heard six-word memoirs from each of Mrs. Nixon's students. The book they created, *Not Quite What We Were Planning: Six-Word Memoirs by Mrs. Nixon's Class,* has been digitized and can be seen at sixword-memoirs.com/schools.

Kathy Najimy ("Fat feminist girl . . . famous, who knew?" p. 77) is a TV and film actor, who may be best known as the voice of Peggy Hill on *King of the Hill.*

Craig Newmark ("The inevitable triumph of the nerds," p. 109) is the founder of Craigslist. We asked Craig if he meant to write "nerd" (singular) when he sent in his memoir, to which he replied, "No, plural for sure—lots of us."

Franz Nicolay ("Let me entertain you. No, please!" p. 57) plays the accordion and the piano in World/ Inferno Friendship Society and keyboards in The Hold Steady.

Dr. Mehmet Oz ("Healed with steel, then got real," p. 199) is vice-chair and professor of surgery at Columbia University and the health expert on *The Oprah Winfrey Show*. He has authored three *New York Times* bestsellers, including *You: The Owner's Manual*, has a regular column in *Esquire* and *Reader's Digest*, and performs over 300 heart operations annually. He says his memoir is "about my beginnings as a heart surgeon and then transition into books and TV."

Sir Michael Parkinson ("My next guest is Jesus Christ," p. 143) is an English broadcaster and journalist best known for his interview-based radio show *Parkinson*.

Tony Parsons ("Wanted: stories heard on mother's lap," p. 24) is a British journalist and the author of the novel *Man and Boy,* which has been published in thirty-nine languages and won the British Book of the Year Prize in 2001.

DBC Pierre ("Hm. Are we nearly there yet?" p. 192) is an author and won the 2003 Booker Prize for his book *Vernon God Little*.

Ed Ramsell ("We both reached for the gun," p. 86) is a retired high school teacher and principal and now an amateur astronomer, photographer, and long-range target shooter. About his memoir, he says, "This phrase summarizes my experience in a forty-year career in public and business education, training, and administration:

Get there firstest with the mostest. Especially the first-est when dealing with kids."

Andy Raskin ("Ate, prayed, and loved, but differently," p. 216) is the author of *The Ramen King and I: How the Inventor of Instant Noodles Fixed My Love Life*. About his memoir, he says, "After a particularly bad breakup, I joined a support group where I was asked to write letters to God about all the relationships I could remember. I wasn't sure whether I believed in God, so I chose instead to write to Momofuku Ando, the inventor of instant ramen. It was a random choice, based on my love of Japanese food, but eventually I got wisdom back from Ando that led me to a healthy relationship. In particular, he taught me that, behind my romantic failures—and I suspect, all unhappiness—is a chronic self-unacceptance that Ando called the Fundamental Misunderstanding of Humanity."

Andy Richter ("Being nice. Having fun. Getting better," p. 113) is a comedian, actor, and announces on *The Tonight Show with Conan O'Brien*.

Rob Riggle ("I love my big, big balls," p. 151) is a comedian who's appeared everywhere and a TV and film actor who's appeared on *The Office, Arrested Development,* and *The Hangover.* He may be best known as correspondent for *The Daily Show with Jon Stewart.*

Marcus du Sautoy ("Eureka! Margin too small for proof," p. 166) is one of Britain's leading scientists, known for making mathematics more fun and easier to understand. He was host of the TV show *Mind Games* on the British channel BBC 4.

Eric Simonoff ("People like the books I like," p. 169) is a literary agent for William Morris Endeavor Entertainment, where he represents Pulitzer Prize winners Jhumpa Lahiri and Edward P. Jones, among others.

Carol Smith ("Across the street, the generations repeat," p. 227) is a social worker living in New Jersey. About her memoir she says: "After our oldest daughter spent seven years in college and graduate school in

Boston, we never imagined she would move back to our small town. To our delight, she not only returned, but when she discovered the Victorian house across the street was for sale, she and her husband purchased it. Our day may start with an unexpected visit and a hug from a grandson before he heads off to school. When my husband returns from work, he often hears the voice of his granddaughter yelling 'Pop-Pop.' Glancing out of our bedroom window, we can see our three grandchildren fighting, laughing, and playing."

Maya Stein ("Ex-girlfriends make the best literary material," p. 34) has published two collections of personal essays, *The Overture of an Apple* and *Spinning the Bottle,* and a collection of poetry and photography, *Enough Water.* About her memoir, she says, "I was in the midst of a difficult breakup with a girlfriend and in my state of frustration, anxiety, and general confusion, I started writing. I reflected on our most recent sexual encounter, how I'd left feeling a mixture of regret and repulsion and how I knew it would be the last time we'd have sex. It was not a pretty piece, to say the least. But I ended up submitting it to an anthology of writing about sex and love, and it was published a year later."

Gloria Steinem ("Life is one big editorial meeting," p. 100) is a leading voice of the modern feminist movement. She is an author, lecturer, and cofounder of both *New York* and *Ms.* magazines. Steinem spoke these six words at a memorial for Clay Felker, the legendary magazine editor, and agreed this sentiment made a fitting six-word memoir. Her next book is entitled *Road to the Heart: America as if Everyone Mattered,* a book about more than thirty years as a feminist organizer.

Jesse Thorn ("He got to meet his heroes," p. 128) is an NPR radio personality, producer, and host of *The Sound of Young America.* Some of the heroes he's met and interviewed include Terry Gilliam, Bill Withers, and Bob Odenkirk.

Mark Zupan ("Hit me, I'll hit you back," p. 207) is a quadriplegic rugby player who won the gold medal in the Beijing Paralympics. He was featured in the film *Murderball*.

For more backstories, as well as videos from six-word memoir readings across the world, visit sixwordmemoirs.com.

Index

Acting, 12, 81, 82, 121, 187

Age, 1, 5, 8, 24, 38, 43, 52, 55, 63, 65, 75, 113, 121, 128, 130, 155, 157, 163, 164, 165, 176, 178, 190, 198, 201, 211, 215, 218

Alzheimer's, 7, 40, 197

Animals, 26, 32, 34, 47, 69, 79, 84, 106, 114, 118, 123, 125, 127, 138, 143, 196, 204, 207, 209, 215, 228

Art, 6, 7, 15, 21, 23, 70, 72, 78. 142, 149, 157, 173, 184, 204

Bipolar, 55, 90

Bodily functions, 2, 31, 163, 170

Body parts, 6, 7, 17, 20, 25, 36, 56, 67, 87, 94, 97, 102, 137, 141, 150, 151, 172, 178, 187, 192, 194, 198, 205, 212, 218, 221, 222, 226

Boobs, 7, 13, 46, 95, 205, 212

Books, 42, 43, 50, 59, 77, 82, 85, 130, 138, 140, 169, 193, 196, 216, 222

Booze, 12, 23, 31, 47, 56, 106, 110, 111, 115, 122, 143,

150, 155, 171, 172, 174, 194, 215

Career, 2, 5, 7, 9, 14, 18, 22, 23, 24, 25, 27, 28, 37, 38, 39, 53, 57, 68, 72, 83, 88, 99, 101, 126, 134, 140, 148, 157, 167, 169, 201, 202, 203, 216, 218, 226

Chapters and drafts, 1, 42, 59, 73

Characters, 1, 14, 16, 29, 38, 43, 47, 57, 74, 75, 85, 92, 107, 132, 138, 171, 196, 203

Children, 8, 9, 12, 20, 21, 26, 28, 30, 31, 33, 34, 36, 53, 59, 64, 66, 72, 83, 86, 102, 104, 115, 118, 120, 130, 134, 141, 149, 157, 170, 171, 193, 194

Clothing, 14, 18, 66, 110, 145, 155, 163, 165, 194, 198

Coffee, 57, 106, 110, 197

Computers and the Web, 2, 8, 12, 26, 36, 57, 68, 125, 130, 140, 146, 172, 174, 179, 184, 208

Criminal Justice, 9, 16, 75, 89, 104, 155, 157, 176, 208

Dancing, 13, 50, 59, 92, 113, 116, 150, 187, 226

Death, 7, 20, 26, 34, 36, 38, 40, 46, 47, 52, 60, 62, 69, 95, 116, 153, 160, 173, 174, 175, 183, 200

Dick, 126, 128, 211, 226

Diseases, disorders, and disabilities, 5, 7, 20, 39, 40, 49, 55, 59, 62, 74, 77, 79, 83, 86, 94, 95, 101, 117, 121, 146, 147, 149, 150, 154, 155, 161, 170, 187, 190, 197, 200, 212, 214, 216, 218, 224, 226, 228

Divorce, 4, 31, 36, 102, 115, 160, 182

Dreams, 84, 107, 134, 151, 178, 184

Drugs, 139, 167, 185, 208, 212

Fame, 17, 27, 77, 167, 201, 214

Family, 2, 4, 7, 14, 33, 46, 47, 55, 62, 79, 84, 89, 94, 146, 159, 160, 174, 175, 200

Fat, 56, 59, 66, 102, 151, 214

Fear, 7, 62, 201

Fertility, 23, 30, 121, 218

Flowers, 26, 85, 132, 194

Food, 13, 24, 30, 31, 39, 49, 53, 62, 66, 89, 91, 99, 101, 104, 110, 111, 147, 161, 163, 189, 193, 204, 205, 215, 216, 221, 226

Friendship, 3, 28, 29, 52, 73, 75, 170, 173, 179

Gay, 7, 26, 45, 50, 65, 69, 82, 106, 115, 164, 206

Geeks and nerds, 14, 83, 109, 151, 166, 187

Gender, 2, 30, 85, 93, 101, 114

God, 8, 59, 72, 118, 163, 169, 188

Hair, 51, 96, 160, 165, 173

Home, 8, 23, 24, 118, 149, 200, 219

Laughter, 1, 88, 145, 211, 227, 229

Marriage, 4, 8, 14, 18, 19, 22, 26, 38, 53, 56, 61, 70, 73, 79, 82, 94, 102, 130, 134, 141, 143, 155, 161, 167, 170, 182, 183, 189, 190, 206, 213, 215

Math, 65, 125, 166

Military, 9, 111, 143, 207

Money, 4, 24, 56, 66, 92, 95, 164, 180

Music, 4, 21, 22, 27, 62, 64, 70, 102, 115, 126, 140, 157, 204, 227

Nudity, 40, 50, 153, 194

Obama, 31, 142, 150,

Parents, 7, 33, 40, 42, 43, 45, 52, 60, 62, 69, 79, 80, 115, 116, 120, 123, 128, 135, 150, 156, 171, 173, 176, 187, 200, 201, 218, 222

Pickles, 30, 39, 170

Places, 4, 16, 20, 23, 33, 46, 54, 74, 120, 137, 145, 146, 154, 178, 184, 189, 203, 205, 207, 211, 213, 219

Politics, 31, 33, 76, 83, 92, 110, 150, 216

Porn, 18, 56

Prom, 18, 64, 110

Psychopharmacology, 4, 8, 39, 126, 146, 218

Race, 12, 13, 17, 58, 79, 101, 116, 123, 138

Religion, 9, 16, 45, 49, 52, 55, 68, 69, 74, 88, 99, 121, 130, 137, 140, 146, 147, 153, 161, 171, 176, 189, 201, 216

School, 7, 9, 29, 84, 88, 135, 166, 179, 186, 198, 227

Sex, 2, 14, 18, 20, 55, 63, 64, 74, 92, 107, 111, 131, 166, 178, 194, 208, 228

Shoes, 37, 41, 46, 90, 146, 198, 200, 226

Social Networking, 19, 37, 86, 120, 138, 157, 170, 194

Sports, 12, 28, 52, 107, 113, 167, 184, 200, 211

Suicide, 46, 47, 60, 143

Teaching, 7, 16, 75, 113, 174, 213

Television, 75, 121, 132, 138, 147, 149, 192, 200

Travel, 20, 23, 24, 56, 79, 147, 160, 163, 167

Vegetarian, 13, 91, 115, 207

Virginity, 2, 28, 178

Writers, 62, 82, 85, 101, 121, 180, 212

Writing, 1, 8, 10, 16, 18, 34, 39, 42, 44, 49, 50, 57, 59, 61, 70, 78, 121, 131, 145, 149, 161, 173, 196, 204, 213, 216

Yoga, 32, 154, 173

 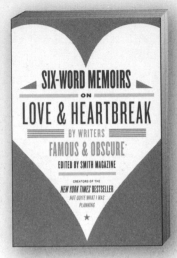